Life in the Forest

By Connor Stratton

www.littlebluehousebooks.com

Little Blue House is distributed by North Star Editions:
sales@northstareditions.com | 888-417-0195

Produced for Little Blue House by Red Line Editorial.

Photographs ©: sirtravelalot/Shutterstock Images, cover; Matt_Gibson/iStockphoto, 4; Creaturart Images/Shutterstock Images, 7 (top), 24 (top right); SueTot/Shutterstock Images, 7 (bottom); FotoRequest/Shutterstock Images, 9; Allen.G/Shutterstock Images, 11 (top); Ondrej Prosicky/Shutterstock Images, 11 (bottom), 24 (bottom right); LuCaAr/iStockphoto, 12, 24 (top left); MEGiordano_Photography/iStockphoto, 15; Baranov E/Shutterstock Images, 17; legna69/iStockphoto, 18, 24 (bottom left); BMJ/Shutterstock Images, 21; Jim Cumming/Shutterstock Images, 23

Library of Congress Control Number: 2019908249

ISBN
978-1-64619-021-8 (hardcover)
978-1-64619-060-7 (paperback)
978-1-64619-099-7 (ebook pdf)
978-1-64619-138-3 (hosted ebook)

Printed in the United States of America
Mankato, MN
012020

About the Author

Connor Stratton enjoys hiking through forests, spotting new animals, and writing books for children. He lives in Minnesota.

Table of Contents

Forest Animals

The forest has many trees.

Many different animals

live in the forest.

Foxes and wolves live in the forest.

Their bodies are covered with fur.

Both animals hunt for their food.

Many kinds of birds live in the forest.

A woodpecker has a beak that is strong and sharp.

The woodpecker uses its beak to poke holes in trees.

Eagles and owls live in the forest too.
Eagles have wide wings, and owls have large heads.

Big Animals

Bears are big animals that have thick fur.

Bears eat many different kinds of plants and animals.

Moose are big animals
that grow antlers on
their heads.
Moose eat plants,
but they do not eat
other animals.

Cougars are big cats that live in the forest.

Cougars are fast runners. They often hunt deer, but sometimes they eat smaller animals.

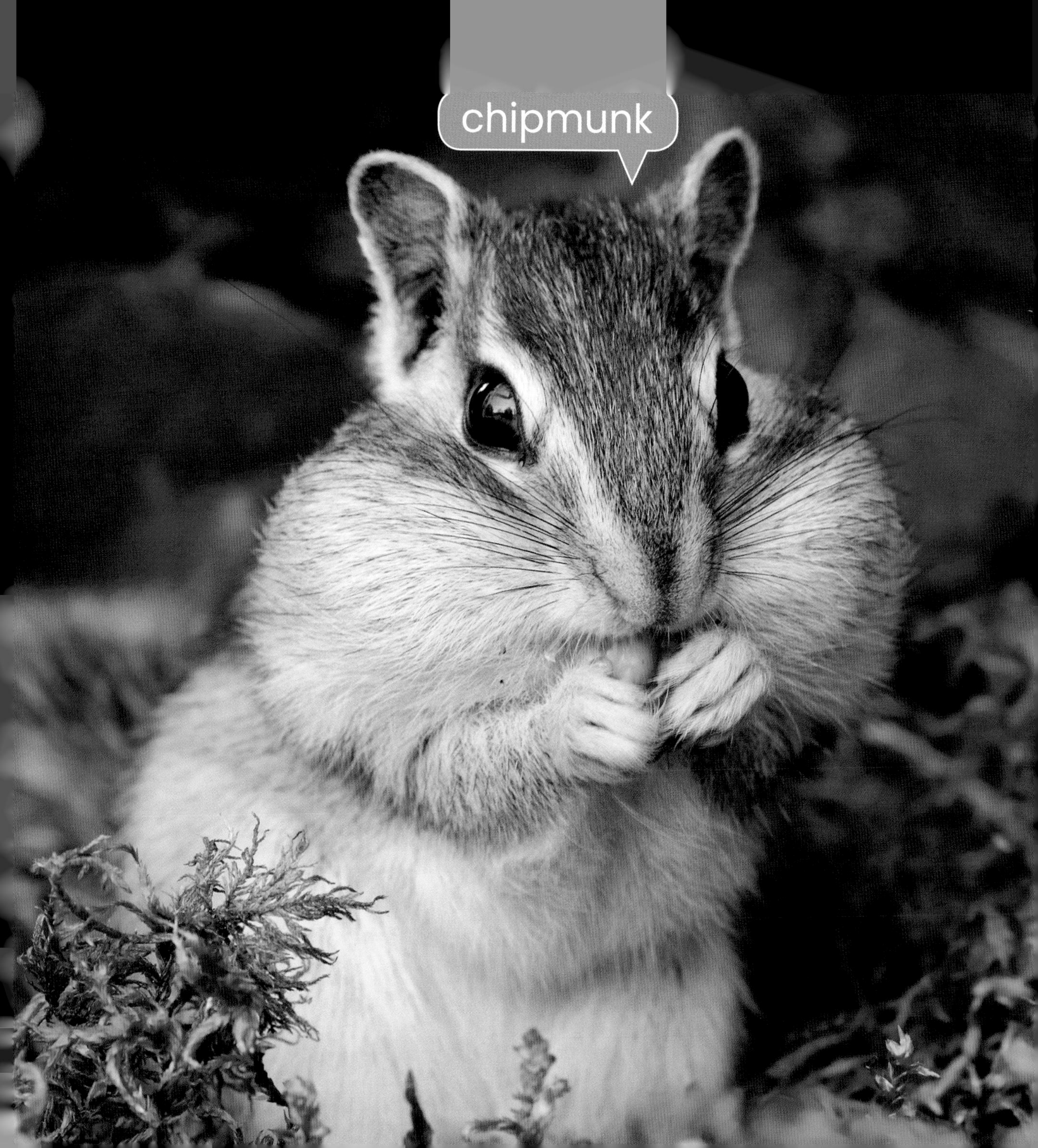
chipmunk

Small Animals

Chipmunks are small animals that live underground. Chipmunks eat nuts and seeds.

Beavers are small animals that live near lakes and rivers.
They chew wood from trees to build their homes.

Hares are small animals that live in the forest. Hares can quickly hop from place to place.

Glossary

bear

fox

chipmunk

owl

Index